Piano • Vocal • Guitar

# the music glee
## season two
### volume 5

| Page | Song |
|---|---|
| 2 | Thriller / Heads Will Roll |
| 11 | Need You Now |
| 16 | She's Not There |
| 18 | Fat Bottomed Girls |
| 23 | P.Y.T. (Pretty Young Thing) |
| 29 | Firework |
| 35 | Baby |
| 43 | Somebody to Love |
| 49 | Take Me or Leave Me |
| 55 | Sing |
| 61 | Don't You Want Me |
| 65 | Do You Wanna Touch Me? (Oh Yeah!) |
| 71 | Kiss |
| 76 | Landslide |
| 83 | Get It Right |
| 90 | Loser Like Me |

Series Artwork, Fox Trademarks and Logos
TM and © 2010 Twentieth Century Fox Film Corporation.
All Rights Reserved

ISBN 978-1-45840-281-3

**HAL•LEONARD® CORPORATION**
7777 W. BLUEMOUND RD. P.O. BOX 13819 MILWAUKEE, WI 53213

For all works contained herein:
Unauthorized copying, arranging, adapting, recording, Internet posting, public performance,
or other distribution of the printed music in this publication is an infringement of copyright.
Infringers are liable under the law.

Visit Hal Leonard Online at
www.halleonard.com

# THRILLER/HEADS WILL ROLL

**HEADS WILL ROLL**
Words and Music by KAREN ORZOLEK,
NICHOLAS ZINNER and BRIAN CHASE

*\* Recorded a half step lower.*

Copyright © 2009 Chrysalis Music Ltd.
All Rights in the U.S. and Canada Administered by Chrysalis Songs
All Rights Reserved Used by Permission

**THRILLER**

Words and Music by
ROD TEMPERTON

* In the recording, the chords continue to change over the L.H. ostinato.

Copyright © 1982 RODSONGS
All Rights Controlled and Administered by ALMO MUSIC CORP.
All Rights Reserved  Used by Permission

# NEED YOU NOW

Words and Music by HILLARY SCOTT,
CHARLES KELLEY, DAVE HAYWOOD
and JOSH KEAR

# SHE'S NOT THERE

Words and Music by
ROD ARGENT

Copyright © 1964 MARQUIS MUSIC CO. LTD.
Copyright Renewed
International Copyright Secured   All Rights Reserved

# FAT BOTTOMED GIRLS

Words and Music by
BRIAN MAY

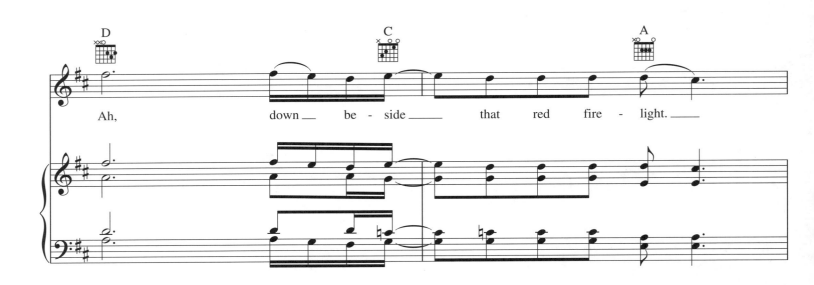

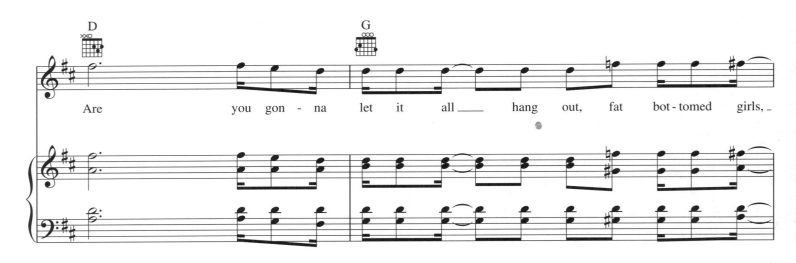

© 1978 QUEEN MUSIC LTD.
All Rights for the U.S. and Canada Controlled and Administered by BEECHWOOD MUSIC CORP.
All Rights for the world excluding the U.S. and Canada Controlled and Administered by EMI MUSIC PUBLISHING LTD.
All Rights Reserved   International Copyright Secured   Used by Permission

# P.Y.T.
## (Pretty Young Thing)

Words and Music by QUINCY JONES
and JAMES INGRAM

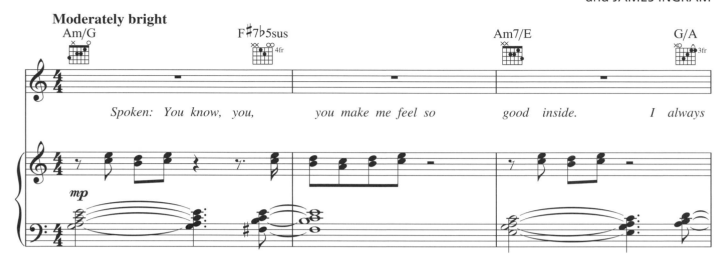

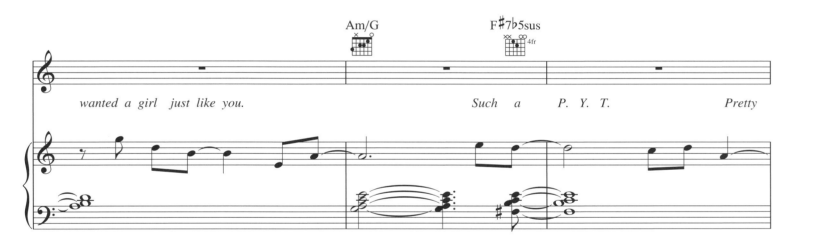

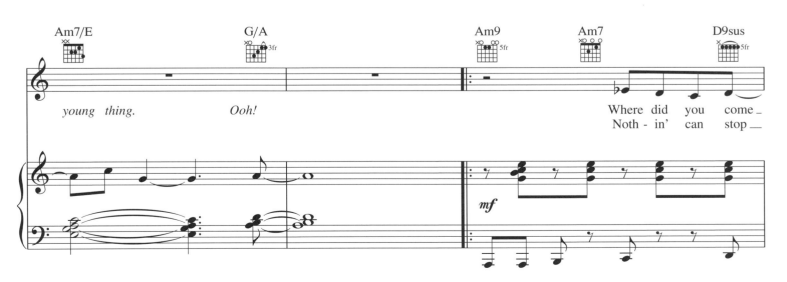

Copyright © 1982 Yellowbrick Road Music (ASCAP) and Warner-Tamerlane Publishing Corp. (BMI)
Worldwide Rights for Yellowbrick Road Music Administered by BMG Chrysalis
International Copyright Secured   All Rights Reserved

# FIREWORK

Words and Music by MIKKEL ERIKSEN,
TOR ERIK HERMANSEN, ESTHER DEAN,
KATY PERRY and SANDY WILHELM

© 2010 EMI MUSIC PUBLISHING LTD., PEERMUSIC III, LTD., DAT DAMN DEAN MUSIC, 2412 LLC,
WB MUSIC CORP., WHEN I'M RICH YOU'LL BE MY BITCH and DIPIU MUSIC PUBLISHING S.R.L.
All Rights for EMI MUSIC PUBLISHING LTD. in the U.S. and Canada Controlled and Administered by EMI APRIL MUSIC INC.
All Rights for DAT DAMN DEAN MUSIC and 2412 LLC Controlled and Administered by PEERMUSIC III, LTD.
All Rights for WHEN I'M RICH YOU'LL BE MY BITCH Controlled and Administered by WB MUSIC CORP.
All Rights Reserved   International Copyright Secured   Used by Permission

# BABY

*Words and Music by JUSTIN BIEBER,
CHRISTOPHER STEWART, CHRISTINE FLORES,
CHRISTOPHER BRIDGES and TERIUS NASH*

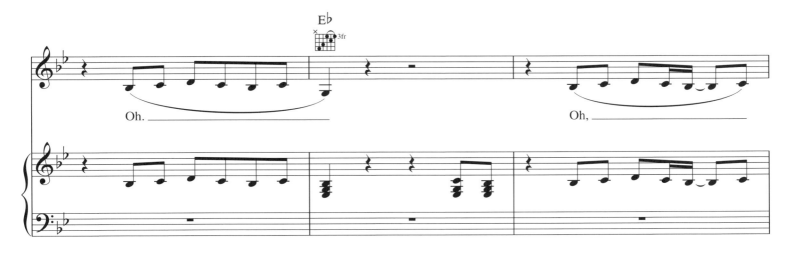

Copyright © 2010 UNIVERSAL MUSIC CORP., BIEBER TIME PUBLISHING, RZE MUSIC PUBLISHING, SONGS OF UNIVERSAL, INC.,
HAVANA BROWN PUBLISHING, LUDACRIS WORLDWIDE PUBLISHING, INC., WB MUSIC CORP. and 2082 MUSIC PUBLISHING
All Rights for BIEBER TIME PUBLISHING and RZE MUSIC PUBLISHING Controlled and Administered by UNIVERSAL MUSIC CORP.
All Rights for HAVANA BROWN PUBLISHING Controlled and Administered by SONGS OF UNIVERSAL, INC.
All Rights for LUDACRIS WORLDWIDE PUBLISHING, INC. Controlled and Administered by EMI APRIL MUSIC INC.
All Rights for 2082 MUSIC PUBLISHING Controlled and Administered by WB MUSIC CORP.
All Rights Reserved   Used by Permission

# SOMEBODY TO LOVE

Words and Music by JUSTIN BIEBER, HEATHER BRIGHT, RAY ROMULUS, JEREMY REEVES and JONATHAN YIP

Copyright © 2010 UNIVERSAL MUSIC CORP., BIEBER TIME PUBLISHING, STAGE THREE SONGS, B-RHAKA PUBLISHING,
SONY/ATV MUSIC PUBLISHING LLC, PLEASE ENJOY THE MUSIC, WB MUSIC CORP., SUMPHU and PRODUCTS OF THE STREET
All Rights for BIEBER TIME PUBLISHING Controlled and Administered by UNIVERSAL MUSIC CORP.
Worldwide Rights for STAGE THREE SONGS and B-RHAKA PUBLISHING Administered by BMG CHRYSALIS
All Rights for SONY/ATV MUSIC PUBLISHING LLC and PLEASE ENJOY THE MUSIC Administered by SONY/ATV MUSIC PUBLISHING LLC, 8 Music Square West, Nashville, TN 37203
All Rights for SUMPHU and PRODUCTS OF THE STREET Controlled and Administered by WB MUSIC CORP.
All Rights Reserved   Used by Permission

# TAKE ME OR LEAVE ME
from RENT

Words and Music by
JONATHAN LARSON

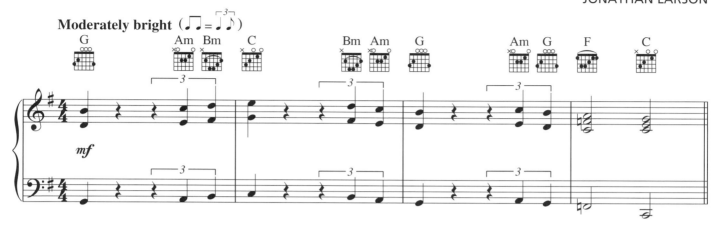

Copyright © 1996 FINSTER & LUCY MUSIC LTD. CO.
All Rights Controlled and Administered by UNIVERSAL MUSIC CORP.
All Rights Reserved  Used by Permission

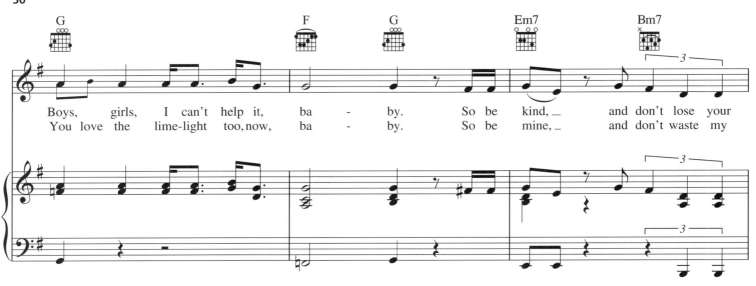

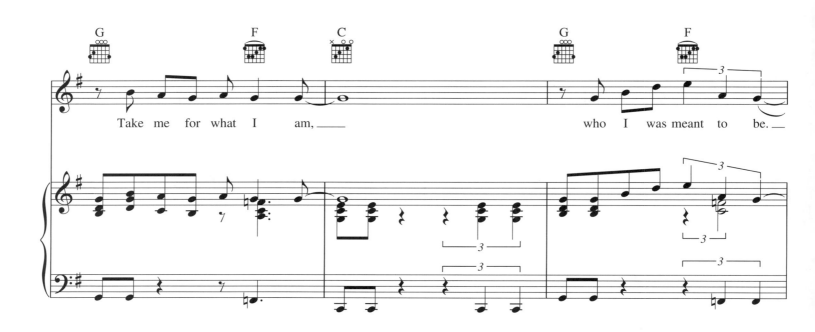

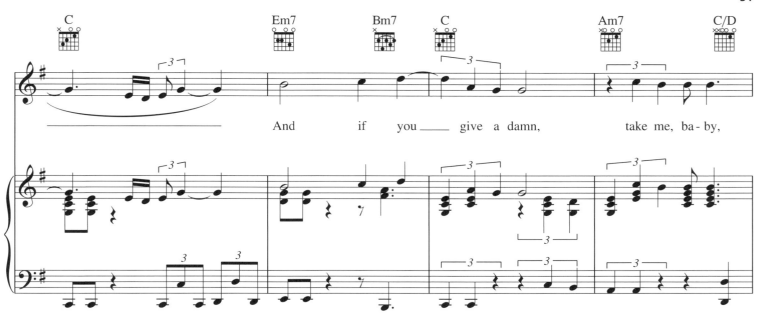
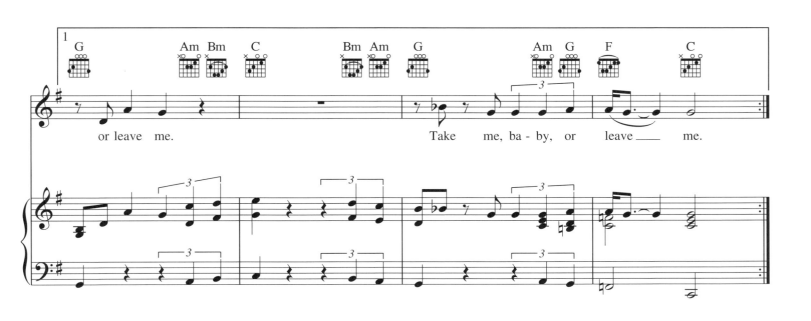
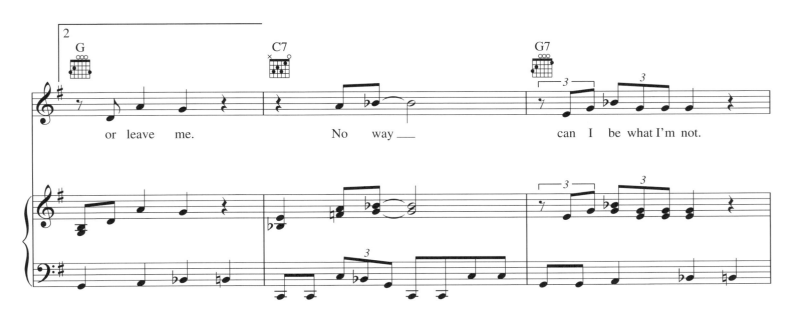

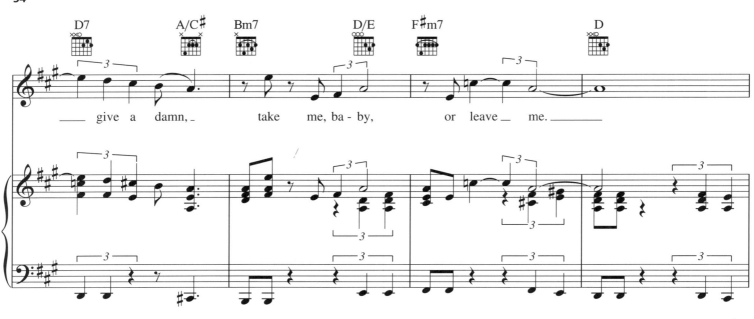
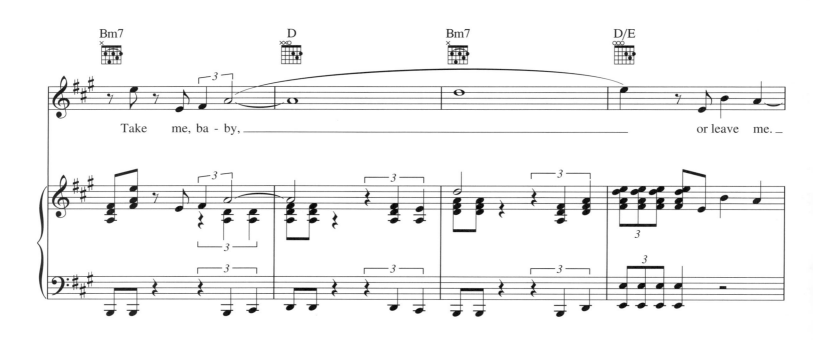
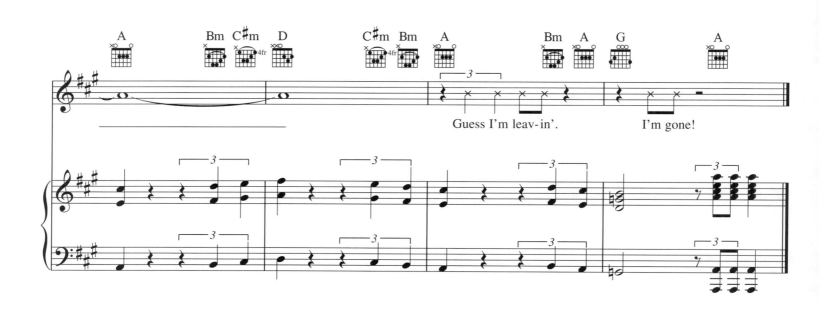

# SING

Words and Music by FRANK IERO,
RAY TORO, MIKEY WAY
and GERARD WAY

*With energy*

Sing it out, boy, you've got to see what tomorrow brings.
Sing it out, boy, they're gonna sell what tomorrow needs.
Sing it out, boy, you've got to be what tomorrow needs.
  boy, before they kill what tomorrow brings.
You've got to

© 2010 Better Living Industries (BMI)
All Rights Reserved   Used by Permission

*Additional Lyrics*

3. I was working as a waitress in a cocktail bar,
   That much is true.
   But even then I knew I'd find a much better place
   Either with or without you.

4. The five years we have had have been such good times,
   I still love you.
   But now I think it's time I live my life on my own.
   I guess it's just what I must do.

# DO YOU WANNA TOUCH ME?
(Oh Yeah!)

Words and Music by GARY GLITTER
and MIKE LEANDER

* Recorded a half step lower.

Copyright © 1973 UNIVERSAL MUSIC CORP. and BMG GOLD SONGS o/b/o Palan Music Publishing Ltd.
All Rights for BMG GOLD SONGS Controlled and Administered by BMG CHRYSALIS
All Rights Reserved   Used by Permission

# KISS

Words and Music by
PRINCE

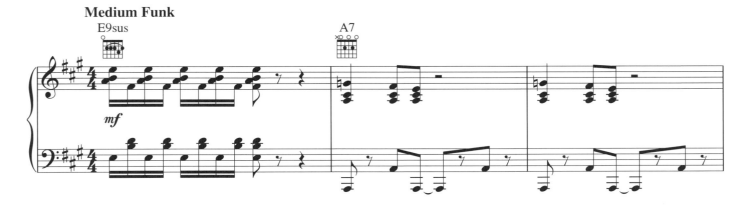

Copyright © 1986 CONTROVERSY MUSIC
All Rights Controlled and Administered by UNIVERSAL MUSIC CORP.
All Rights Reserved   Used by Permission

# LANDSLIDE

Words and Music by
STEVIE NICKS

# GET IT RIGHT

Words and Music by ADAM ANDERS, NIKKI HASSMAN and PEER ASTROM

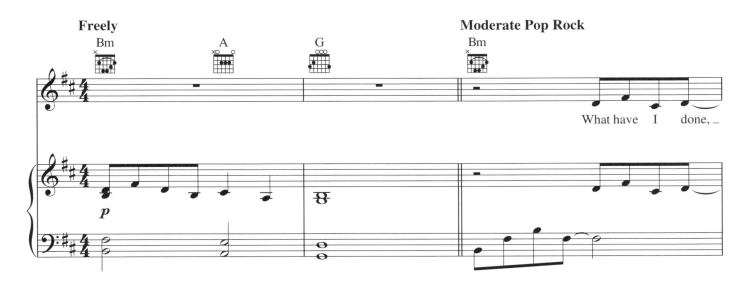
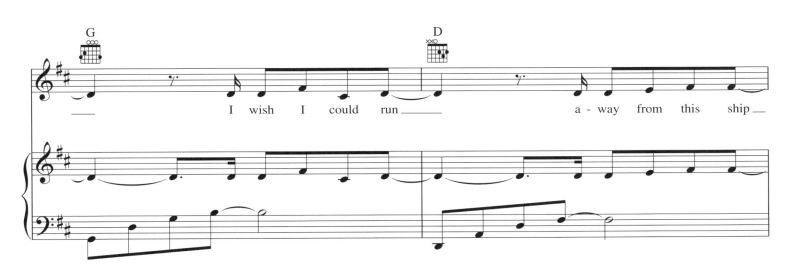

Copyright © 2010 T C F Music Publishing, Inc.
All Rights Reserved   Used by Permission

# LOSER LIKE ME

Words and Music by ADAM ANDERS, PEER ASTROM, MAX MARTIN, SAVAN KOTECHA and JOHAN SCHUSTER

Copyright © 2010 T C F Music Publishing, Inc., Fox Film Music Corp., Mr. Kanani Songs, EMI April Music Inc. and Maratone AB
All Rights for Mr. Kanani Songs Controlled and Administered by EMI April Music Inc.
All Rights for Maratone AB Controlled and Administered by Kobalt Music Publishing America, Inc.
All Rights Reserved   Used by Permission